paige tate & CO.
www.paigetate.com

Published in 2016 by
Paige Tate & Co.
An Imprint of PCG Publishing LLC
3610 Avenue B
San Antonio, TX 78209
email: reagan@paigetate.com
www.paigetate.com

All rights reserved. No part of this publication may be reproduced or transmitted in any form or by any means, electronic or mechanical, including photocopy, recording or any information storage and retrieval system, without permission in writing from the publisher.

Scriptures taken from the Holy Bible, New International Version®, NIV®. Copyright © 1973, 1978, 1984, 2011 by Biblica, Inc.™ Used by permission of Zondervan. All rights reserved worldwide. www.zondervan.com The "NIV" and "New International Version" are trademarks registered in the United States Patent and Trademark Office by Biblica, Inc.™

ISBN: 978-1944515379

introduction

Dearest Friends,

Do you know that you are doing a great job? I feel as you open this book it's a truth that needs to be spoken over you and whispered in your ears. It's something that God wants you to hear every day, but far too often we let the noise of the world around us overpower His voice. We fall into the lie that "We don't have time for a quiet time." (Trust me, I have four kids - quiet is not in my vocabulary!) God is not surprised by your messes, your tired soul or your busy schedules. He knows it is hard for you to find quiet moments to spend with Him. However, just by opening these pages, you are taking a really key step. You are showing up.

It's my desire that through the pages of this book the word of God will become even more alive than ever for you. As you pause to think, pray and create, I hope that you would understand how much you are loved and cherished. I hope you walk away each day with a renewed love for God's love letter to you and better understand the importance of your role as a mother.

Thank you for taking the time to dive deeper into your relationship with our Creator. Just as our hearts as mothers explode with joy when our child reaches for our hand or wants to snuggle in close - our Father feels the same love for us. He is anxiously waiting for you to grab His hand and snuggle in a little closer to Him.

Enjoy this precious time finding moments of peace in your day to turn your eyes toward Him!

All my love,

Kara-Kae James

**"Then I will ever sing in praise of your name and
fulfill my vows day after day."
Psalm 61:8**

Are you like me? Do you clean maybe, once every few months? Come on, be honest!! It feels a little pointless doesn't it? The second you mop the floors someone spills an entire gallon of milk and moments after you wipe down the bathroom to perfection a certain two-year old decides to decorate with shaving cream and toilet paper.

Housework feels like a never ending battle. And don't even get me started on the laundry! I would rather just go buy my husband new underwear than have to do One.More.Load. A never ending battle.

But what if we looked at it as a gift?
Bear with me a moment, I know what you're thinking.

How in the world could housework be a gift?
And trust me, I'm a little angry with myself for even proposing it.
But what if? What if we took a step back and saw each thing for what it truly is?
What if we ACTUALLY did everything without complaining or arguing?
Could you IMAGINE??

What if we made messes and enjoyed life instead of worrying about how much cleaning we may have to do? What if?

What if we chose to embrace each mess as JOY and truly embraced each one? What if we didn't cringe at the thought of play dough, finger paint and sand boxes?

I'm a very type-A person, so messes tend to be stressful for me. But when I take a moment to see the bigger picture, oh man. It's so much better than the stress my feeble mind creates.
A few weeks ago, I was cleaning in a frenzy (you know what I mean, those days where you must

---

clean everything??). As I was scrubbing from top to bottom and completely ignoring my kids who were begging me to play, I made it to our back door. It's a glass door overlooking our back patio and yard. As I sprayed Windex on it and started scrubbing away in a huff, I noticed something. I saw two tiny handprints with a little smudge between them. I paused. I imagined my one year-old with her hands and nose pressed against the glass excited about a bird, squirrel or just a leaf blowing by. I couldn't help but laugh picturing her so filled with joy, and then my tears started flowing.

God spoke to my heart in that moment and reminded me that this was a masterpiece. Designed by Him. He gave me that precious girl, who is perfectly unique and wonderful. I could see her tiny, dirty finger prints. The prints that God made and knew every little curve by heart. I put away my spray bottle and left the prints as a reminder. Praising God that I have tiny fingerprints to clean.

Embrace the beauty of each day, and allow those dirty fingerprints to be a masterpiece for the life that God is designing for you.

RESPONSE

PRAYER

TODAY'S SCRIPTURE

"Yet the LORD longs to be gracious to you; therefore he will rise up to show you compassion. For the LORD is a God of justice. Blessed are all who wait for him!"
Isaiah 30:18

The idea of "rest" is not something that is practiced much in our culture anymore. We are fast-paced, red-faced, non-stop people. We are women, we are moms. The raisers of the tiny humans. We do what we believe is expected of us. If we sit down with a speck of dust in sight or a single dirty dish in the sink, we let those little voices in our head taunt us that we shouldn't rest.

In Isaiah 30, God is speaking to the children of Judah. They are foolish and rebellious. They are seeking approval elsewhere and turn away from God in their own fear. God calls them back to Himself. They learn the lesson of trust which is still such a difficult lesson for God's children to learn. I battle with trust daily because I turn to the idols and people in my life for approval just like Judah did.

This is what the Sovereign Lord, the Holy One of Israel, says:
"In repentance and rest is your salvation, in quietness and trust is your strength, but you would have none of it." Isaiah 30:15

I feel like the Lord is saying this directly to me. I'm hiding behind my dust bunnies and seeking the approval of how many people say my kids are cute. "Rest in Me", He says. I can't take 5 minutes to slow down. "Repent of your flesh", He cries out. Instead, I brush off my sin as human nature and continue to fall over and over. "TRUST ME", He pleads with me. My flesh wants nothing to do with it.

Repent. Rest. Quiet. Trust. Confidence in God quiets and stills the soul. It brings peace to a storm of fear. Trust in God brings rest to our plans and sets our eyes on Him. He fills us with salvation and strength.

When we keep reading in Isaiah 30,
"Yet the Lord longs to be gracious to you; therefore He will rise up to show you compassion. For the Lord is a God of justice. Blessed are all who wait for Him!" Isaiah 30:18

He longs to show us compassion, it's not just something He has to do because He's God. Even when we continue to fail Him daily and hide behind our fears and dust bunnies. It's time to put down our idols of housework, measuring up or comparison. It's time to truly trust in the One who brings us refreshing rest!

And remember - rest in Him does not mean there is an absence of disturbance in your life, especially with those little noise makers you are raising. It simply makes the noise more glorious!

DAY
03

TODAY'S SCRIPTURE

"Carry each other's burdens, and in this way you will fulfill the law of Christ. If any of you think you are something when you are nothing, you deceive yourselves."
Galatians 6:2-3

There was this season of motherhood where I was sort of a hermit. We were going through a ton of change. And in the midst of all the change, we were desperately trying to figure out our sweet son, who was leaving us completely lost at the end of every day. We knew something wasn't quite right and we were heartbroken that we couldn't seem to figure out how to make him happy.

Going out with the kids was like running a marathon. It was physically and emotionally exhausting because I was in constant prevention mode. Always trying to leave the house prepared for whatever crisis would befall us. Always on the watch for triggers that would bring on a meltdown that we would be unable to recover from. There were several times I had no choice but to leave a cart of groceries and walk out. Bless you dear grocery store workers for picking up after me.

Finally, I just decided...it was just easier to stay home. It was easier to be home where people wouldn't be staring as my child had fits of rage over the fact that he was too cold or heard a noise he didn't like. I would imagine their inner dialogue, and it would haunt me later as I lay in bed.

Home: where I could hide in the bathroom and cry if I needed to, instead of losing it down aisle 5 in front of complete strangers. Hiding just felt easier. But it was also very, very lonely.

Finally, I humbled myself enough to confess to dear friends that we were in a very desperate place and didn't know what we were doing AT ALL. I was supported, cared for, and so loved. Friends dropped packages with magazines, chick flicks, and chocolate. Friends listened on the phone as I hysterically cried and vented and fell apart. Friends prayed over me. Friends brought cups of Starbucks and books.

Friends came.

Friends. Community. A rich love that covered the dark place…the miry pit I couldn't pull myself out of, or so I felt.

Sometimes it seems easier…cleaner…prettier…to just contain your mess in the privacy of your own home. But the real beauty happens when friends come and sit with you smack dab in the middle of your big, stinky mess. That's real. That's genuine. And THAT is gospel.

"Bear one another's burdens, and thereby fulfill the law of Christ. For if anyone thinks he is something when he is nothing, he deceives himself." Galatians 6:2-3

It's hard to pull back the curtain that reveals what's really going on behind the scenes, and it's not always convenient or comfortable to step into someone's pit and help pull them out. But, it's beautiful to realize what God does when we bear one another's burdens.

Healing. Hope. Joy. Jesus.

RESPONSE

PRAYER

**"Finally, be strong in the Lord and in his mighty power. Put on the full armor of God, so that you can take your stand against the devil's schemes."
Ephesians 6:10-11**

I'm a fighter, a bit of a scrapper really. I had a big brother, so growing up I had to learn to be a little tough and fight for myself. I remember so many times having wrestling fights with my brother. He was so much bigger than me, so he would just sit on me. I was worthless when he did this. And if he was smart enough to tuck in my arms so I couldn't get a punch in, I didn't stand a chance.

Sometimes it feels like the enemy is sitting on top of us, arms tucked in and we are just fighting to breathe. It feels like we don't stand a chance and that he has complete victory over us, doesn't it? I know I feel like that a lot.

But the truth? The amazing, beautiful truth is you are already victorious. We are not fighting for victory in this life - in Him, the outcome is always victory. We are not warriors fighting toward victory, we are warriors fighting in victory. Yes, there are real battles in this life and He has provided us with the tools to fight against the enemies of this world. As moms, we are on the front lines every day fighting for our children's hearts, our marriages, our businesses, our relationships.

I don't know what battle you are fighting today, but I want you to know that you are not alone. Each one of us is fighting, some of us struggling just to breathe. But there is grace here. The battle has been won, the victory is His and through Him we can fight every battle in victory!

I want you to be fully armed for battle so nothing this world throws at you can take you down.

You are mighty.
You are victorious.
You are a warrior.

It's my prayer for Retreat that you walk away feeling fully equipped to use the battle armor God has provided for you.

Take that grace with you this week.

TODAY'S SCRIPTURE

"For we are God's handiwork, created in Christ Jesus to do good works, which God prepared in advance for us to do."
Ephesians 2:10

We see the world through a variety of filters. If you scroll through your Instagram feed, you see hundreds of beautiful images carefully edited, brightened and filtered. Blemishes can be covered and corrected. The messy parts behind you can be blurred out and unseen.

Don't you wish you could wake up and choose a filter to put on yourself of how you will be seen? Maybe you're a bit tired so you'll go black and white. Or you can pick something that brightens your eyes and brings out your skin tone. The way we view ourselves is quite different than all those people liking your latest selfie.

Let's do an exercise together. I want you to grab a piece of paper and go to the mirror. What is the first word or phrase that comes to mind when you look at yourself? What is that nagging lie you believe each time you look at who you are as a mom? I want you to write that on your paper.

Now comes the fun part: put a big mark through it!

Ask God how He sees you. What are the truths he speaks over you and into your heart? Below the lie you wrote, I want you to write a truth about who God says you are. He sees you through the filter of Christ. You are covered by His blood and redeemed. You are not that lie that you crossed out. That lie is nailed to the cross. You are His.

It's time to start seeing yourself through the filter of Christ.

WHO DOES HE SAY THAT I AM?
Fearfully & wonderfully made (Psalm 139:14)
His treasured possession (Deut. 7:6)
Complete (Col. 2:10)

The apple of His eye (Psalm 17:8)
Chosen (1 Peter 2:9)
His friend (John 15:15)
Redeemed (Romans 3:24)
An heir (Romans 8:17)
Set free (Galatians 5:1)
Holy & blameless (Eph. 1:4)
The salt of the earth (Matthew 5:13)
His ambassador (2 Corinthians 5:20)
Blameless (1 Corinthians 1:8)
Adopted as His child (Ephesians 1:5)
Overcoming (1 John 4:4)
Victorious (1 John 5:4)
Hopeful (Ephesians 1:12)
A new creation (2 Corinthians 5:17)

Safe (1 John 5:18)

"For we are God's workmanships, created in Christ Jesus to do good works, which God prepared in advance for us to do." Ephesians 2:10

The mirror can be our worst enemy.
We tend to believe and live in the lies the mirror tells us.
The lies that the enemy haunts us with.

God sees the real you.
You are covered by grace.
Covered by the filter of Christ's blood.
You are redeemed.

Sometimes it can be hard to wake up and live each and every day, each and every moment viewing ourselves through His filter. Maybe you haven't showered in days, and the thought of even looking at yourself in the mirror is torture. He still sees your heart. Maybe you feel like a failure because of how you yelled at your kids last night. His grace covers you. Or the tension between you and your husband is unbearable. He heals and redeems.

It can be so easy to fall into those lies that the enemy whispers in our ears. As women and moms, we are such easy targets. We are emotional and exhausted. We are weary and weak.

It is time to push the lies aside.
Walk in the truth of who HE says you are.
Live in freedom!

RESPONSE

PRAYER

"Be devoted to one another in love.
Honor one another above yourselves."
Romans 12:10

I was sitting there on the couch at the end of what, at the time, seemed like the longest day in the history of days, and I sent a text message that went something like this:

"Girls, please pray. I'm having a really rough day. I put the kids to bed an hour early because I couldn't take it another second. I just peed for the first time since this morning and still had a baby in my lap while doing so. Sitting on the couch and can't stop crying. I haven't felt this bad in a long time."

On those days, I have a group of girls that I immediately turn to. They understand my struggles and are walking through this season of life with me. They know my battles. I know their daily struggles and how to pray for them. It's a community where judgment and comparison are not allowed. And when I send them a message like that (which happens A LOT), they immediately jump to my rescue with scripture, prayer, and encouragement. A lot of times they just show up on my doorstep with a yummy drink and a hug. They are my people. They get me.

Because there are those days that rock you to your core. You reach your breaking point, and all you can do is scream. Unfortunately, my pillow doesn't get it. I can scream all I want into it and get nothing in return. My pillow doesn't sympathize with me and my pillow just doesn't get it. And even though my husband is my best friend, he doesn't get it either.

That's where community comes in. Real, genuine, comfortable, perfect community.

It's my community that gets me through my harder-than-hard days.

They point me to Jesus and remind me to thrive through each day as a mom.
Do you have those friends in your life that you consider family?
The ones that your children run straight into their house without even knocking and know

right where the good snacks are? The ones that you can text in your darkest moments or cry on their voicemail when you've hit your lowest point? The ones that will drop anything for you? You know that kind who will help themselves to whatever is in your fridge and are happy to walk through the good and bad seasons of life with you.

FIND YOUR PEOPLE.

It can be so difficult to form deep, meaningful relationships when you are a busy mom. Your days revolve around your kids, and you're in a constant state of being the housekeeper, cook, taxi driver, homework checker, alphabet teacher, and hiney wiper. You're pulled in a million directions, but it's your people that will pull you in the right direction. Don't have those people? GO FIND THEM! Invite someone for coffee, or send an email. Take that step, and you may discover your best friend is out there somewhere feeling just as lonely as you!

BE INTENTIONAL.

Be the friend that you would want someone to be to you. When you have a hard day, what lifts your spirits? An encouraging text message? Finding your favorite drink on your front porch? A hilarious picture to make you laugh? Get to know your people on a deeper level.

Proverbs 17:17 says that "A friend is always loyal, and a brother is born to help in time of need." Be a friend that loves at ALL times, even when it's you that needs the love. And be a SISTER. A friend as close as family. God has given us one another to walk through times of adversity with, do not try to do it alone!

devoted to one ANOTHER in Love

ROMANS 12:10

TODAY'S SCRIPTURE

"But you are a chosen people, a royal priesthood, a holy nation, God's special possession, that you may declare the praises of him who called you out of darkness into his wonderful light."
1 Peter 2:9

The crisp fall leaves crackle beneath my feet as I push the stroller up the hill toward the park. I settle into a bench far from anyone and snuggle the baby into me as the big kids run off to play. This is the only few minutes of quiet I might get the entire day, so I close my eyes and soak in the warm sun and cool breeze on my face.

As I open my eyes, I take in the sights around me. The beauty of the trees, the sun reflecting off my daughter's bright blonde locks and the laughter of children all around. It's all so very beautiful. I see other moms clinging to their moments of peace while they watch their children play and wonder what's on their hearts today. Are they hurting? Are they struggling? Where are they in their motherhood journey?

One mom looks exhausted. She probably hasn't showered in a few days and her shirt is covered in what is most likely either spit up or someone's breakfast. Her eyes tell the story as she stares off, probably dreaming of a hot shower where no one flushes a toilet or throws army men at her.

Then I look over to the mom chasing her three boys. She seems to have more energy than they do. How does she do it? Where's her cape, because surely she must have some sort of super powers. No one actually has that kind of energy, do they? As I sit there with barely enough energy to hold the baby in my arms, I wonder how she's doing it.

I also think of each of you as I sit. Yes, you. Sitting behind your computer. And you reading from your phone at 3am while you nurse your baby. You with your third cup of coffee and it's still not enough. You on your 7th load of laundry and still no end in sight.

What is in your heart today? In the midst of the chaos, the mess, the never-ending needs? Are you able to find delight in the madness of it all? Do you know that you are enough? You're not just enough, you are CHOSEN. Chosen to be a mother, a wife, a sister and a friend. You are

chosen by God. His possession. And because of this - He's called you out of the darkness. The darkness that can overtake motherhood. He hovers over the chaos and welcomes you into His beautiful light.

I think we have a tendency to view the messy, sticky parts of our lives as a failure or an inconvenience. But those pieces are part of His perfect plan. God didn't create children to come out being clean and knowing how to put their toys away. That was His plan all along.

Cling to those messy, sticky parts. Put the kids to bed tonight and allow the mess to sit, while you rest in His truth and the fact that you are exactly the mom He created you to be. Enjoy childhood for exactly what He created it to be: childhood.

Maybe you're in an "easy season" where you are finding margin in your day for yourself, or maybe you haven't had a second to yourself in months. Maybe you're that mom about to fall asleep on the park bench, or the one chasing your kids wearing your supermom cape. Either way, you are chosen. Since He has chosen you, choose to embrace and adore the perfect season He has given you. God doesn't make mistakes and He hand picked you to be the mom to your kids.

Choose joy.
Embrace the messy, sticky parts.
Invite Him to be a part of your wild, chaotic lives.
Your chaos is a promise of His perfect plan for your life.

He wants you to run to Him. To lay the dirty laundry, the sticky floors and the greasy hair at His feet. Your life is no secret to him, He knows. It's not out of His concern or His control. You are fully and completely covered by His grace and love even when you're covered in spit up, mud and peanut butter sandwiches.

Now, sweet sisters, it's our turn to show others the goodness He offers in the chaos!

RESPONSE

PRAYER

"There is a time for everything, and a season for every activity under the heavens."
Ecclesiastes 3:1

Sometimes I battle with change. I am a woman of routine, lists and schedules. Nothing makes me happier than a perfectly organized playroom and a color coordinated closet. I think there is something about it that makes me feel safe. When things are in "order", my life feels stable.

But that's not reality.

The reality is that the playroom is a complete disaster 5 minutes after I have every toy in it's properly labeled tub (as if my 2 and 3 year olds can read?). The clothes are most likely in piles in the laundry room ready to be thrown in for a good fluff when I need a certain outfit. And that really cute meal plan I made on that super cute chalkboard? None of those meals happened and the last time my kids had a bath? Oops, we won't even go there. Reality hurts sometimes.

I find myself saying
"this is JUST a season"
at least once a day.

I realize how awful that sounds!

Our seasons are made to be beautiful, a precious gift from God. Not just something we have to "get through" so we can move on to something new and better!
Honestly, yes, my season is very challenging right now.
But, there is HOPE and TRUTH that makes it so much easier.

GOD HAS A PLAN FOR EACH SEASON.
Maybe your season is incredibly painful as you've just lost another baby from a miscarriage.
Maybe your season is filled with joy because your daughter just rode her bike by herself.

Maybe you are battling with a house full of sick kids and you feel like you'll never get a break. Maybe you feel like all you do is run your kids from one activity to the next and you're looking at the mom with 3 kids in diapers, begging her to enjoy it because it goes too fast.

Seasons can seem much prettier from the outside. When you are standing in the dead heat of summer, you feel like you can't breathe and you're just dying for winter. For a break. Then winter begins to wear on you and you see someone else in their spring and yearn to be there.

God does have a plan for each of you. He has a perfectly unique plan for your season. Wishing that you had someone else's spring will do nothing but make your winter even colder.

EMBRACE & ENJOY your season

There is a TIME for everything

ECCLESIASTES 3:1

TODAY'S SCRIPTURE

"I have told you these things, so that in me you may have peace. In this world you will have trouble. But take heart! I have overcome the world. "
John 16:33

I collapsed into my favorite corner of the couch and wrapped myself tightly in my favorite blanket. It was silent. A silence I felt like I hadn't heard in days, even weeks. "Lord, I don't think I can do this again tomorrow", I whispered into the darkness that surrounded my warm sweater blanket and me. My kids had all been sick for nearly two weeks, and I was at the end of my rope. I couldn't take another day filled with non-stop crying, fevers, exhaustion, and disobedience due to the exhaustion. Everything seems to come out in those hard times, most of all: the ugliness and impatience of my heart.

This isn't what it was supposed to be like. Why do children get sick, why is motherhood so hard, why do I let myself down and feel like I'm letting down everyone around me?

In the midst of the tears that were forming in my eyes, the truth was whispered back to me:

"In this world, you will have trouble, but take heart, I have OVERCOME the world."
(John 16:33)

He has overcome
the heartache,
the illness,
the disappointment
and even my shortcomings.

Doesn't that just feel like a huge weight was lifted off of your shoulders? All the worries and troubles of the day just fade away.

Raising children in this world can be terrifying, overwhelming and downright heartbreaking.

But He has OVERCOME the world.

People often confuse the life as a Christ follower to be deliverance from suffering. But the truth is, following Christ gives us deliverance IN our suffering. Even the most devout Christ followers will still face unimaginable pain. The Bible tells us we WILL face trials and tribulations. Even Jesus faced suffering, and a lot of it! We often fear to talk of our struggles, but Paul tells us to boast in them! God uses our hard times to shape us and grow us. He has overcome it all, and given us the power to overcome through Him!

In this scripture, Jesus tells us to take heart in the midst of our tribulations. To be of good cheer. To be filled with a deep peace. I don't know about you, but this is HARD. As you lean over your sleeping child and take their temperature for the 20th time in the night and it still reads 103.6. As you sit and listen to your child's teacher tell you that he has a learning disability. As you hold the hand of your best friend while they place the body of her baby in the ground. As your husband walks out leaving you to raise your three babies alone.

You feel worry, despair, anger, hurt, frustration and defeat. Peace is not even in your vocabulary.

Maybe your trials are just the exhaustion of caring for your kids, potty training or endless timeouts. Whatever it may be for you, I urge you to run into His arms and fall into that unshaken, absolute and endless peace that can only come from Him.

"That is why I am suffering here in prison. But I am not ashamed of it, for I know the one in whom I trust, and I am sure that He is able to guard what I have entrusted to Him until the day of His return." 2 Timothy 1:12

Sweet sisters, He stands guard over your heart, your children and your marriage to overcome the suffering you face. Allow Him to overcome your world.

RESPONSE

PRAYER

"Finally, brothers and sisters, whatever is true, whatever is noble, whatever is right, whatever is pure, whatever is lovely, whatever is admirable- if anything is excellent or praiseworthy- think about such things."
Philippians 4:8

"Authenticity" has become one of those trendy buzz-words. I've gotten to the point that it makes me cringe when I see it. I'm weary of hearing people in an outcry about being real and using social media as their soapbox. We boast about our weakness to fit in a trendy culture of authenticity when we should be boasting in our weakness as a cry to be more like Jesus.

Your thoughts and words carry a great amount of weight. You can run to social media as a place to vent about your kids, spouse, and your home or you can think about the weight of your words first. In Philippians, Paul gives an incredible example of what our captions should say.

"Finally, brothers and sisters, whatever is true, whatever is noble, whatever is right, whatever is pure, whatever is lovely, whatever is admirable—if anything is excellent or praiseworthy—think about such things." Phil. 4:8

Every time we go to speak, to post or to comment we should think about such things.

You can learn a lot from someone by what they are saying, and better yet, what they aren't saying. I have a dear friend who taught me to read between the lines of what people say and how a lot of times it's a cry to be seen or loved without even saying much. We have to open up our hearts and learn to read the heart behind what people are saying. We don't have to post a picture on social media of a dirty kitchen floor with a caption of "my life totally stinks" for others to understand what motherhood is about.

So, what are people REALLY saying in their words? How can we see a need for us to love others deeply online and carry that over into real life? I think this is a truly beautiful aspect of social media. A close friend may not disclose the trouble in her marriage but she may run to Facebook to vent her issues. You can take this opportunity to reach out and love her. Read between the captions of what may be a desperate cry for help.

Finally, dear sisters, think before you publish. Is it true, noble, right, pure, lovely, admirable, excellent and praiseworthy? Post about those things.

TODAY'S SCRIPTURE

"My flesh and my heart may fail, but God is the strength of my heart and my portion forever."
Psalm 73:26

I have this scripture hanging in our playroom, and I look at it constantly through the week. Every time I read it, I can't help but wonder if there was a typo in that scripture. When I read this for myself, it says "My flesh and my heart WILL fail.". There's no maybe about it. It will happen and does happen. I fall short on a consistent basis. I'm a failure. My heart fails me, and my flesh fails me.

BUT GOD.

There's the silver lining. But God. Scripture constantly provides that beautiful shining hope. We are humans, we fail....BUT GOD. Today I will fail my kids, BUT GOD. Today I will fail my husband, BUT GOD. Today I will fail God, BUT GOD.

I find myself thinking, "I will fail and I'm not good enough, so what's the point of even trying?". What if God thought that about us?? He knows we will fail, but He continues to chase after us, cover us with His grace, pick up the pieces and turn us into something extraordinarily beautiful. That's what Him being your strength and portion are.

Every time I lose my temper, He is my strength.
Every time I doubt myself, He is my portion.
Every time. Every single time.

That's a promise that I need a reminder of daily. He is my strength because I can't do it on my own. He is my portion because I'm simply not enough.

Precious sisters, rest in that promise today. Walk into your week knowing that even though you WILL fail, He is your strength and your portion. Through Him, we are the extraordinarily amazing mothers he calls us to be.

Be intentional in the way you are a mother, wife, and friend this week.

Our challenge for you: allow His grace to cover your flesh so that you can show grace to your children. Let them see you fail, and that you have to reach out to Him for strength. Let the "But God" ring in your heart and know that you CAN do it all through Him and Him alone.

RESPONSE

PRAYER

TODAY'S SCRIPTURE

"They say of the LORD, 'He is my refuge and my fortress, my God, in whom I trust.' "
Psalm 91:2

As moms, it's really easy to fall into a lifestyle of fear. We are responsible for these tiny human lives. It can be pretty terrifying when you think about it. We are protectors. We guard our children physically, emotionally and spiritually. We do everything we can to protect them from heartbreak and broken bones. But we can only protect them so much, can't we?

God doesn't call us to a life of fear, but of freedom. He wants us to live freely in the confidence that we are His and under the protection of His mighty hand. It's easy to get caught up in doing it all, and forgetting the reason we are moms and the reason we are raising them. They are actually His and He can't fully use them until we extend them to Him.

Motherhood is a beautiful thing because we get to reflect our heavenly Father and his image as we parent. We imitate so many characteristics of God as moms, but it's easy to let the fear creep in and forget that we are not the ultimate protector of our family - He is.

When I go through seasons of fear, I turn to Psalm 91. I sit and re-write this scripture for our family. I love the peace and freedom I find in those words. "We, the James family, we live in the shelter of the Most High! We find rest in the shadow of the Almighty. We declare this about the Lord: He alone is our refuge and place of safety. He is our God and we trust Him!" I do this for the entire chapter. It's like an anthem for our family and a reminder where our protection rests.

Are you hovering and fearful of every move? Or are you parenting with open arms to Christ, knowing that pointing them to Him is the only way you can really protect your children? I'm not saying it's okay to let your kids jump off the roof of your house, but I am saying, as daughters of the King, we can walk fearlessly through motherhood. What a precious truth that is!

I pray you find peace and freedom in that today. If you are walking through motherhood in fear, it's time to let those chains fall. Allow Christ to become your protection.

He is my
REFUGE
& my
fortress

PSALM 91:2

TODAY'S SCRIPTURE

"Love the Lord your God with all your heart and with all your soul and with all your mind and with all your strength. The second is this: 'Love your neighbor as yourself.' There is no commandment greater than these."
Mark 12: 30-31

She gently knocked on the garage door, and only because her hands were full with the milkshakes she had just stopped to get both of us on the way over. Normally, she would have just walked right in. That's the kind of friend she is. An open door, bring-me-a-milkshake kind of friend. She sat across from me at my kitchen table and poured out her heart while I worked on birthday party decorations for one of my kids.

The hours quickly passed, all too quickly as they always do when we have time to sit together and catch up. After finishing her milkshake, she got up to wash her hands in my kitchen sink. When she sat back down, I remembered how I hadn't done dishes in a few days and a bit of embarrassment came over me.

"I'm sorry about the pile of dishes in the sink," I said quickly, letting that feeling of mom guilt creep in as I realized the smell coming from my sink could knock a person over.

"What dishes?," she replied with a completely straight face.

The two most beautiful words a person could say to me. It hit me. This is life as a mom. She didn't look at my sink and judge me for my pile of dishes or pity me for my poor housecleaning skills. She simply washed her hands in a sink that made her feel at home because hers looked the same way at her house.

She saw past the dirty dishes, straight to my heart.

We talked for hours about how hard it is to manage a home, how we struggle with comparison and how we never feel like we can measure up as a mom, wife and follower of Christ. We poured out our hearts of the passions that God has placed in us and encouraged one another to chase those dreams.

It's moments like that that remind me:

I'm not alone.
I AM doing a great job.
We are in this thing together.

Whether you have that ignores-your-dirty-dishes type of friend, or you're struggling to find a place to fit where you are, this applies to you. We are all in this thing together, and your dirty sink is exactly what ours looks like, too. We are thankful for each of you and that you allow us to pray for you and encourage you!

I wish I could sit across the table over a cup of coffee and tell each one of you how incredible you are and listen to your hearts. Whenever you feel alone, feel lost and feel like no one gets you, remember this.

You are NOT alone.
You ARE doing a great job.
We are ALL in this TOGETHER.

There are so many ways to love someone and let a friend know she's not alone. Maybe it's an understanding smile to the mom at the store with screaming kids. Or helping a friend as she folds 12 loads of laundry. Sending a note to someone who is hurting. Or simply a hug and a kind word letting someone know they aren't alone.

Christ tells us that loving others is as important as loving God. That's an incredibly powerful commandment! How can you love someone this week?

RESPONSE

PRAYER

**"What, then, shall we say in response to these things?
If God is for us, who can be against us?"
Romans 8:31**

I'm not typically a news reader or watcher. I get my news from Twitter and Jimmy Fallon and that's about all I usually have the time/energy for. I logged into Facebook a few days and saw back-to-back news stories about moms who tried to end their own lives and those of the children. One who drove her minivan into the ocean with her children inside and another who succeeded in killing herself and one child from carbon monoxide poisoning in her garage and her 5-year-old son was able to survive.

I only tell you these details to remind you how REAL the troubles of this world are. Because as I was reading those stories with tears streaming down my face, I realized I felt the exact pain those mothers had felt. I had felt that pain that very day. Just a few hours prior to reading those stories of hopelessness, I had felt it. I was at the end of my rope. I couldn't take another minute of being with my children. I had cried to my husband to please come home and let me get away. That's just the raw honesty. We've all been there, haven't we?

Motherhood is incredibly difficult. It's draining, it's exhausting and rarely ever praised. I'm in the season of raising very small children who are constantly needy. They need me at all times, and it can become too much sometimes.

We need to understand and validate the hurting moms around us. We need to know that depression, anxiety and hopelessness are feelings women around us face daily. Maybe you are reading this today and feeling some of these things. I want you to know that the hurt in your heart is heard. What you are feeling is real, and it's okay.

The good news? We have HOPE.

Our HOPE rests in Him alone. Nothing else can get you to the end of an extremely long day. Not a bowl of ice cream or a glass of wine. Not a bubble bath. Not a shopping trip to Target

alone. Although those things are nice (I mean, really nice), they will never fill the void and heal your heart the way that He can.

His love is UNSTOPPABLE.
His love is RELENTLESS.
He will never stop fighting for you.
He pursues you with mercy and grace.

"What shall we say about such wonderful things as these? If God is for us, who can ever be against us? Since he did not spare even his own Son but gave him up for us all, won't he also give us everything else? Who dares accuse us whom God has chosen for his own? No one—for God himself has given us right standing with himself. Who then will condemn us? No one—for Christ Jesus died for us and was raised to life for us, and He is sitting in the place of honor at God's right hand, pleading for us. Can anything ever separate us from Christ's love? Does it mean He no longer loves us if we have trouble or calamity, or are persecuted, or hungry, or destitute, or in danger, or threatened with death? (As the Scriptures say, "For your sake we are killed every day; we are being slaughtered like sheep.") No, despite all these things, overwhelming victory is ours through Christ, who loved us. And I am convinced that nothing can ever separate us from God's love. Neither death nor life, neither angels nor demons, neither our fears for today nor our worries about tomorrow—not even the powers of hell can separate us from God's love. No power in the sky above or in the earth below—indeed, nothing in all creation will ever be able to separate us from the love of God that is revealed in Christ Jesus our Lord." Romans 8:31-39

if GOD is FOR US who can be AGAINST us??

ROMANS 8:31

"For he chose us in him before the creation of the world to be holy and blameless in his sight."
Ephesians 1:4

How often do you find yourself apologizing for messes? Probably at least once a day when your husband walks through the door. On the rare occasion that I cleaned my house, I always grab my husband's hand and march him proudly around the house to point out my successes of the day. A clean floor! A toilet that doesn't have rings around it! An empty sink! Laundry actually hung in the closet instead of piled on the dining room table!

Oh, the successes of motherhood.

What if we were to point out proudly the successes of our messes instead of apologizing for them?

Look! A sticky floor where my 2-year old practiced drinking from a big girl cup. A pile of blocks where the 5 year-old practiced his engineering skills. Kids covered in dirt that had a blast wrestling in the sandbox.

What if we really embraced our chaos as beauty instead of apologizing for it? It can be easy to misunderstand what "embracing chaos" means. This doesn't mean that we throw up our hands and say, "Ok mess! you win!" The blanket statement to "embrace chaos" is not meant to make you feel guilty or even an out for the way you might be "just surviving". It's about so much more than that. It's about truly seeking God right in the craziness of life to thrive in the midst of whatever comes your way. God is not surprised by how rowdy your kids are or how dirty your floors are. This is not news to Him.

So the question is, why are you apologizing for the chaos?
Is it because you're afraid of what someone may think of you?

I found myself apologizing to the FedEx guy recently when he dropped off some packages at my

DAY
15
cont.

house. Was I really THAT worried about what some random person thought of who I am as a mother? The FedEx guy is not the final say in who I am. He doesn't even have a say at all, only my flesh makes that possible.

God is the only say. He's the final answer.
He wraps up our chaos with a beautiful bow.
He CHOSE us. Called us. Without FAULT.

"I will not apologize for my sticky floors and cobweb filled corners.
I will not fall victim to what the world says I am.
I will proclaim victory over my home because this is a sanctuary of salvation.
I am doing holy work.
I am raising up the next generation of God's chosen people and
I will not apologize for the messes that happen in this glorious journey.
I will stand firm in who God says I am and know that this calling of being a mother may be the most important thing for the kingdom that I ever do.
Instead of raising my white flag to my home and my children,
I raise my white flag to Christ alone!
I surrender myself to Christ and will thrive in the calling of who He created me to be."

RESPONSE

PRAYER

TODAY'S SCRIPTURE

"Have I not commanded you? Be strong and courageous. Do not be afraid; do not be discouraged, for the LORD your God will be with you wherever you go."
Joshua 1:9

She clung as tightly as possible to my leg as she watched the other children run around the playground. "Who can I play with, Mommy?", she whispered up to me in a quiet voice. I could see the fear in her eyes, as she was afraid to step out into something new.

"I'm right here with you honey, but you need to go make some friends. You will have so much fun!" I told her as I nudged her to go join the other kids. Off she went, and it wasn't 5 minutes before she ran by waving wildly at me, hand-in-hand with her new best friend. The fear was gone, and she had found true community.

"You are my Hiding Place" has been the theme we are focusing on with this study; let's look at that a little deeper. The Hiding Place is a place of refuge, of shelter, of protection and of peace. Just like you protect your children, God wants to protect you. Further, you would never keep your children locked up as a way to keep them safe from the world around them. You want them to play, learn and have fun with other children. You desire community for them, do you not?

When we seek God as our "Hiding Place", it doesn't mean we should just hide out and go through life alone! God built us for community with other people.

Somehow, it seems that when we become the grown-ups and our playground days are behind us, after we've been burned a time or two, we put up walls. We let fear overwhelm our hearts. Genuine Community is out of arms' reach and we let fear take its place.

Satan wants to keep you in a little box-o-fear. He wants you to stay home, watching Greys Anatomy re-runs and eating your third box of girl scout cookies instead of stepping out of your comfort zone and into community with other believers.

Because you know what happens when you get in community? YOU GROW.

"Be strong and courageous! Do not be afraid or discouraged. For the Lord your God is with you wherever you go." Joshua 1:9

Just like I tell my daughter that I am with her wherever she goes, the Lord tells us the exact same thing!
We have nothing to fear when we are hidden in Him!

So, what are you so afraid of?

It's time to turn off the tv, put down the cookies and step out of your comfort zone. Ask God to bring people your way who will help you experience real community! You'll be amazed what He will do - He is just waiting to bless you!

"The soothing tongue is a tree of life, but a perverse tongue crushes the spirit." Proverbs 15:4

Somewhere between the shattered bottle of fingernail polish all over the bathroom and the toddler using the toilet as her own personal swimming pool, I could feel it bubbling up inside of me. You know that tension you start feeling in your chest and you're pretty sure you might just explode?

I remember back when I was a brand new mom, reading a blog post about how this mom was making it a goal to go all day long without yelling at her kids. I remember that baffled feeling as I read that with a perfect, sweet baby sitting in my lap. I was so green, so fresh, so naive. It blew my mind to think that normal people actually got angry and would yell at their kids. I also remember thinking "Well, I will NEVER do that." You're all laughing right now, huh? My apologies to all of the new moms who's giant, peaceful bubble may have just burst.

The reality is, our children are sinful human beings.
Some of them more sinful than others, am I right?

It's sort of a kick in the gut the first time your child deliberately defies you. You see those little wheels turning in their cute, little head as they lie to you and disobey. It's heartbreaking as a parent. It's in those moments when that bubbly tightness in your chest becomes you totally losing your cool over something so small. It's easy to go from "Mom of the Year" to "Who is this Mom?" in about 2.5 seconds flat.

I do not want to be a parent who crushes the spirit of my children. I want to instruct with gentle words building a beautiful tree of life.

I know this is so difficult to remember when you've repeated yourself 500 times and as you're on your hands and knees scrubbing the fingernail polish off of the floor. You want to give in, let out a scream and show them who is boss.

Let's be a generation who yells less and hugs more.
A generation that speaks truth over our kids.
Who speak life into them.
Let's be moms who lift them up and encourage them.
Let's discipline and show grace with a gentle heart.

Remember: there is grace for this day. There is grace for the child who threw the bottle of nail polish and there is grace for you after you lose your temper. There's nothing your child can do to lose your love and there's nothing you can do to lose the love of your Father.

Be a tree of LIFE today.

RESPONSE

PRAYER

TODAY'S SCRIPTURE

" 'No weapon forged against you will prevail, and you will
refute every tongue that accuses you. This is the heritage of the servants of
the LORD, and this is their vindication from me,' declares the LORD."
Isaiah 54:17

Let's talk about the things we second-guess ourselves on. Our parenting styles, our clothes, our makeup, our food choices...basically everything we do. Confidence is something we might be lacking in our lives. We have the world telling us that we aren't good enough, we aren't pretty enough, or brave enough. I tried to think of areas of my life I am confident in and I struggled to make a list of areas where I truly walk in confidence and freedom.

Insecurity is a funny thing. It's something we all battle with in one way or another -- but doesn't God call us to more? We can be confident in our battles because of the fact that God is in complete control.

But confidence can be a tricky thing, too. There's that balance between insecurity, humility, and confidence that we must walk as women and as followers of Christ. In the book of 1 Samuel, we learned about the story of the wise woman. We didn't even know her name, but what we learned about her in just a few lines of scripture was huge and taught me a lot about confidence. She had the reputation of being a wise and confident woman because of the way she lived her life. I don't know about you, but that's how I want to be known!

I'm not always super confident in my decisions or in my choices as a mom. I, like many of you, second guess myself a lot and wonder if I'm doing the best for my kids. It makes me ache when I hear women say they are just trying to survive and get by through a certain season of their lives. That's the heart that Thrive was born out of, because I know that it must break the heart of our Heavenly Father to hear us just trying to survive a life he has given us with such sacrifice.

So, why aren't we walking confidently into our lives and our daily battles? It's finished, He did it all, and took it all so that we could live abundantly.

This scripture tells us that as children of the King -- it is our inherited right through Him to live

secure. Living in confidence and freedom in the victory He gives us!

God is love and He LOVES you. It's your right to live in security of knowing that truth. We pray you will let that sink into your bones today as you walk in confident victory!

No Weapon FORGED AGAINST You will PREVAIL

ISAIAH 54:17

TODAY'S SCRIPTURE

"But he said to me, 'My grace is sufficient for you, for my power is made perfect in weakness.' Therefore I will boast all the more gladly about my weaknesses, so that Christ's power may rest on me."
2 Corinthians 12:9

I'm a prideful person. I like to be the best and do the best. I want to be the mom with the cutest birthday parties, the most likes on the pictures of my kids, and the best chocolate chip cookies on the block. Can't we all relate to that in one way or another?

In 2 Corinthians 12, Paul challenges us to only boast in our own weakness. That's a tough subject to stomach. We live in a world where self-promotion is the key to success. If we aren't bragging on ourselves and all we are doing, then we fear we will get lost in a sea of success stories and get trampled. Paul mentions a thorn in his flesh to keep him from becoming proud. While many Bible scholars have debated about what that thorn actually was, I think the key point is to remember that no one is above pride. Even Paul, a man who was a devoted follower of Christ, needed to be knocked down a notch or two from time to time. Heaven knows I need that.
I have a thorn in my flesh. I have several of them actually. And I bet you do, too. Those painful things in your life that, although you've prayed over and over for the Lord to remove them, dig deeper and deeper into your flesh as a constant reminder that you are not all that.

So you want to boast? Boast in Christ. Boast in your weakness.

The battles we will face in our lives will be won through our weakness. But hear me, it's not about you at all. Because even boasting in our weakness can become prideful! You may think you can only win battles by being a strong and fearless warrior, but Paul teaches us otherwise. The only thing we need is the grace that Christ offers us. The battles are won by Christ through us and the grace He offers.

"My grace is all you need. My power works best in weakness." the Lord told Paul each time he begged for the thorn to be taken away.

We will win battles because the battles are the Lord's and not ours. When we are weak and

willing to allow Christ to work through us, then we are made strong through Him alone.

Praise God today for your weakness, and thank Him for giving you a thorn to keep you in a place that Christ alone can be victorious through you! Allow His grace to wash over you, cover your pride, and let His strength be all you need today, sweet sisters!

RESPONSE

PRAYER

> ### TODAY'S SCRIPTURE
>
> "But now, this is what the LORD says – he who created you, Jacob, he who formed you, Israel: 'Do not fear, for I have redeemed you; I have summoned you by name; you are mine.' When you pass through the waters, I will be with you; and when you pass through the rivers, they will not sweep over you. When you walk through the fire, you will not be burned; the flames will not set you ablaze."
> Isaiah 43:1-2

Motherhood is overwhelming, demanding and unfulfilling. We are overworked and unappreciated. I don't know how many times I've sent a text to my husband during the day saying, "I'm just so overwhelmed." The dishes never end; the laundry piles up; I run my own business that needs my attention; and I just can't do it all. Not to mention trying to be a great mom and wife all day. It's all just too overwhelming.

But the silver lining is that we don't find our fulfillment in motherhood, we find our fulfillment in Christ alone. It's in those moments that God breathes a little breath of life into me and reminds me that I don't have to do it all or be it all. Everything doesn't have to be in order and fit my schedule. He just wants me to give it to Him and worship Him through everything. I find rest and relief in that, don't you?

There's a song by Jenn Johnson that is my go to worship song when I get that overwhelmed feeling. The first time I heard it, I lost all control of my tear ducts after just the first line. "God, I look to You, I won't be overwhelmed". A light bulb went off and I realized I was doing it all wrong. I was getting myself to the point of being overwhelmed and THEN I was looking to God for help. Instead, I should rise every day, look to HIM first and then I won't be overwhelmed.

I can't get enough of this scripture in Isaiah of God reminding us that we are HIS. He has called our name and He will not let us drown. He knows we will get in over our head, but He's right there with us. He won't let us get overwhelmed when we look to Him!

Don't allow the pressure of an overwhelmed life leave you with an underwhelmed soul! God, I WON'T be overwhelmed. Give me the vision for what you want me to do and how you want me to raise these children you've entrusted me with.

Over the past year this song has quickly become my motherhood anthem. Let these words wash over your soul today and find peace and rest in worship and surrender to Him. Him, the only one that can erase the overwhelm and bring complete peace.

Don't
FEAR
FOR I HAVE
Redeemed
You

ISAIAH 43:1

"Rather, clothe yourselves with the Lord Jesus Christ, and do not think about how to gratify the desires of the sinful nature." Romans 13:14

I used to go shopping all the time before kids, just to try clothes on. Not even very often would I buy, but just trying on things was fun for me. I would take piles of clothes into the dressing room just to play dress up and enjoy the feel of the new clothes. Once in a moment of weakness, young and just out of college, I went on a shopping spree with a friend. I ended up spending nearly a thousand dollars on clothes. My husband still jokes with me about that frivolous shopping trip twelve years later.

Although, I learned my lesson in that shopping spree, sometimes I still feel the tug toward the worldly desires. The world tells us constantly -- "You NEED this! You'll be happy with that!". Maybe it's that new flashy iPad or an upgraded minivan. Or maybe it's just that daily cup of coffee from the local coffee shop.

I love the way The Message writes this scripture in Romans 13:11-14:

"But make sure that you don't get so absorbed and exhausted in taking care of all your day-by-day obligations that you lose track of the time and doze off, oblivious to God. The night is about over, dawn is about to break. Be up and awake to what God is doing! God is putting the finishing touches on the salvation work He began when we first believed. We can't afford to waste a minute, must not squander these precious daylight hours in frivolity and indulgence, in sleeping around and dissipation, in bickering and grabbing everything in sight. Get out of bed and get dressed! Don't loiter and linger, waiting until the very last minute. Dress yourselves in Christ, and be up and about!"

How easy is it as moms to get absorbed and exhausted in our daily obligations that we forget about the reason we are doing all of these things? We become oblivious to God and His work in our lives, but it's time to wake up! We need to step into His dressing room to clothe ourselves in His salvation. Make your entire life about Him, wrapped in the presence of the Lord. We

become distracted by the next shiny object or thing that will "make us happy" when He is the only thing that will ever satisfy.

"Instead, clothe yourself with the presence of the Lord Jesus Christ. And don't let yourself think about ways to indulge your evil desires." -Romans 13:14

RESPONSE

PRAYER

TODAY'S SCRIPTURE

"Jesus answered, 'I am the way and the truth and the life. No one comes to the Father except through me.' "
John 14:6

Let's spend some time today looking at survival mode vs. thriving, and how survival mode can wreck our identity in Christ. We throw this around a lot because it's our vision and the foundation of Thrive Moms, but what does it look like to really thrive vs. survive?

Survival mode is failing to understand God and His word. It shows a lack of trust in God and His promises to us. Our need for the "survival mode" goes back to the beginning, to the place it all started for mankind – in the garden. God created us to have dominion over all of His creations. He created this crazy intimate relationship with man that we simply can't fully understand until the day we are reunited with Him again in Heaven.

The Bible talks in Genesis about God walking in the "cool of day," which in Hebrew is a term for the breath of God. God and Adam were so close, they were interwoven more intimately than a man and woman in marriage. They were one in spirit.

So, we get this picture of what we were created to live like. Thriving, intimately with God.

UNTIL SIN. Sin entered the picture, and so did survival mode. Survival mode wrecks our identity and warps our relationship with Christ. What does survival mode look like? It's different for everyone. It's kind of like an art form. I could give ten people a blank canvas and ask them to create the same thing and it would come out so differently from each person. Survival mode looks the same way.

We begin to believe the lies that the world tells us, we begin to believe that "survival mode" is okay because life is hard. But we were created for ABUNDANT life. Sin creeps in and constantly tells us that it's okay to just survive, that our identity lies in what the world says about us. But living is not based on our stuff, our jobs, our kids, and our marriage.

Survival mode is abusing the purpose God created you for. Real living is when our lives are anchored in Him.

So, how do we thrive and find our identity in Him alone? God left us His word as a road map to Him. We can't thrive in this life until we grow to know Him deeper. He gave us His word and the greatest gift of all -- HIS SON. The cross creates a bridge from survival mode to truly thriving in life with Christ.

In John 14:6 Jesus said, "I am the WAY, the TRUTH and the LIFE." That's a prescription for how to thrive. HIM. He is the way. He is the Truth. He is the LIFE. He's the way to leave survival mode behind and step into a thriving, intimate life with God. Jesus didn't come into this world to just survive, and we were made to be new every day -- just like Him.

Thriving in relationship with Him overflows into all aspects of our life. He wants something so sweet for us in motherhood -- to thrive in the chaos and live freely in that calling. To stop abusing our purpose by clinging to strongholds. To find our identity in Him alone so that we can leave our survival tactics and false identities behind and reach only to Him.

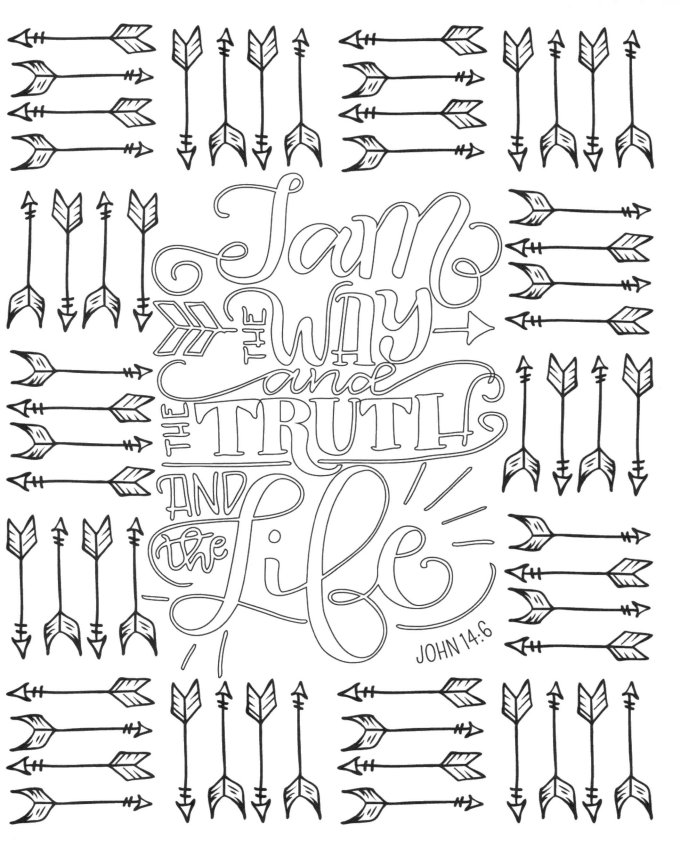

I am the Way and the Truth and the Life

JOHN 14:6

TODAY'S SCRIPTURE

"Shouts of joy and victory resound in the tents of the righteous: 'The LORD's right hand has done mighty things!' "
Psalm 118:15

I was sitting in the recliner rocking the baby to sleep (or at least attempting to) when I heard the rustling of tulle from the other room. The clickity-clack of tiny plastic heels shuffled across the wood floor toward me. I turned to see two proud little faces beaming with joy at their oversized princess dresses and layers of jewels. Tiny crowns adorned the tops of their blonde heads and the now not-sleeping baby giggled in delight at the sight of them.

"Mommy, play us a song! We need to DANCE!"

It's a sentence we hear often in our home filled with girls. They love to turn on music and watch their dresses twirl beautifully around them. I love the part in the scripture Psalm 32:7 of how He "surrounds us with songs of victory". The imagery in these words is beautiful. Just like the image in front of me of carefree, joyful dancing.

Our homes become chaotic, overwhelming and can even become a burden. But because of our salvation we have complete and total joy. Victory. We may fail miserably as moms each day, He is Victorious. We may lose our temper with our husbands, He is Victorious. We may serve Cheetos and M&Ms for dinner (again…), HE IS VICTORIOUS.

"Songs of Joy and Victory are sung in the camps of the godly." - Psalm 118:15

Our God is good, He's bigger than any of our failures and He took on our shortcomings at the cross. He overcame it all so that we can fill our home with songs of joy and victory! Even in our weakest moments, we can find joy in Him. No matter what is going wrong or how much you fail today, your home is a place where joy and victory can be shouted from the rooftops. Allow His sweet melody to sing into your heart. Let the baby skip a nap to enjoy a princess dance party (or a mighty warrior party with your little men!).

Embrace the precious life and moments you've been given. REJOICE in the victory we have in Him!

RESPONSE

PRAYER

TODAY'S SCRIPTURE

"He heals the brokenhearted and binds up their wounds."
Psalm 147:3

This world is full of people with broken hearts, broken spirits, and broken relationships. It was all part of the fall of man, the separation between God and man. It created a deep separation between each of us, too.

Jesus understood rejection and broken relationships. He was betrayed, misunderstood, and rejected by even his closest of friends. In Hebrews 4:15 the Bible says that Jesus is able to empathize with our weaknesses. He knows our hurt because He was hurt, too. When I walk through difficult seasons in community, I always hear that whisper in my ear of "I understand" from Him. When the world misunderstands us, Jesus understands us. And just like a mother caring for a hurt child, Christ bandages our wounds, too.

Broken relationships can be a painful place in our hearts. A place that bitterness and hurt can harbor for many years. You will have disappointments and hurt in relationships. It's part of living in a broken and fallen world. You will hurt others, and be hurt.

But the good news? We are not defined by our relationships, failures, or rejection of others. We are only defined by our relationship with God. We are His, born into NEW life with Him, given every blessing from Him and accepted in Jesus. God has equipped and prepared our hearts to walk through any season of life. We can either walk in our own flesh, basking in our hurts and disappointments, or we can walk in His power. He's given us His armor to guard our hearts and fight our battles.

Sisters, if you are hurting because of broken community, be encouraged. Maybe a hurt has you scared to open up and let people in. Maybe you've done the hurting and you don't know how to apologize. Maybe you're clinging to something that happened in the past and it's keeping you from finding genuine community. God promises to be with you through it all.

He will never leave you. He's your comforter and sustainer. Overcoming hurt takes a lot of prayer and a lot of prayer and focus upon the truths He has given us. Broken relationships are painful, but our God is so gracious and wants to give us amazing community we can be ALL IN! Seek Him today and ask Him to fill your life with that "all in" community.

he heals the BROKENHEARTED and binds up -their- Wounds

PSALM 147:3

TODAY'S SCRIPTURE

"You prepare a table before me in the presence of my enemies.
You anoint my head with oil; my cup overflows."
Psalm 23:5

I remember so vividly the day I sat on my back porch with my face in my hands weeping and feeling so defeated. I had been battling postpartum anxiety and depression for what seemed like forever. My kids had been neglected, my marriage felt the weight of it and I physically hurt from the battle within.

They tell you to "pick your battles" with your children. As a mother of several small children, I have to admit that's some advice I cling to, almost on the daily. But what about when it comes to your life? You don't get to just "pick your battles," since they can come at you in numbers and hit you from every direction. Sometimes the weight of the world comes crashing down around you, and you have no choice in which battle you want to take on.

The battle in your marriage.
The battle with a sick child.
The battle with postpartum illness.
The battle with the work/life balance.
The battle with a special needs child.

There are battles all around, and most likely you are fighting a battle of some sort in your life right now. Maybe more than one.

Sister, the battle is real. So very real.

But there is hope and truth in the battles we face.

The Lord doesn't just blindly send you out into battle. He doesn't send you anywhere He hasn't already been. "He prepares a table for me in the midst of my enemies". (Psalm 23:5) He isn't just there in the middle of your battle, He prepares a feast for you. If you're anything like me, a feast

is not something easy to prepare. ESPECIALLY in the midst of chaos! But God is right there in the middle of our battles with a giant turkey, rolls the size of your face and more pies than Marie Callendar, just waiting for us.

Even in the midst of my darkest battles, I hear that quiet voice whispering,
"I'm right here in this with you. Join Me at the table. I am your Hiding Place. I protect you from trouble. I surround you with songs of victory."

Ladies, suit up and grab your fork. We're going to battle.

TODAY'S SCRIPTURE

"For we are God's handiwork, created in Christ Jesus to do good works, which God prepared in advance for us to do."
Ephesians 2:10

I sat on one of those sink-to-the-floor type of couches in a room filled with boxes of tissues, 90s decor and a wall lined with bookshelves. I couldn't believe I was sitting there in front of a "shrink" for the first time, fighting the tears back and sinking deeper into feeling like a failure just by being in that room. Just weeks before, I had given birth to my third child and I felt like my world was crashing in around me. I sat there thinking about the incredible blessings God had given me, the two year-old, one year-old, and newborn babies at home. I loved them so much and I knew how incredibly blessed I was, but I couldn't shake that feeling that I wasn't good enough and God had messed up by giving them to me.

I sat trying to explain this to my counselor. I told her how people told me I was a rock star, that if anyone could do it -- it was me. And how those words that were meant for encouragement actually brought harm to me. I was comparing myself against an image of a better version of me. I let it defeat me and break me.

In that season I realized that I don't have to compare myself to a model in a magazine, a famous figure, or even the perfectly groomed mom at the park. Comparison can creep in even when I'm looking to myself and what I feel like I should be. It's so easy for us as moms to slip into a defeated state of comparison. We see that mom on Instagram (you know the one I'm talking about), her life seems so perfect and her kids always look adorable. Don't you know that she's human too, and just because she chooses to show the beautiful parts of her life doesn't mean there's not a mess behind that, too?

COMPARISON: INSPIRED OR DEFEATED?
When we look at another person or look at who we want to be we can either be inspired or we can be defeated. There's a couple of questions I want you to ask yourself today when you run across a mom at the grocery store who looks like she stepped out of Vogue.

1) Do I desire to grow closer to Christ because of what I see in this person or do I find myself feeling defeated?

Maybe by seeing that mom, you are inspired to go home and do some laundry so you can get out of your sweatpants. Maybe you're inspired to dust off your treadmill and lose some of that weight that makes you unhappy. Or maybe you feel defeated and bury your head into the nearest package of Oreos. It's usually easier to retreat to a place of defeat.

2) What is the foundation of my defeat?

Is there something deeper happening here? When you are looking at someone else in a state of comparison and feel defeated, is there an issue in your own life that you need to deal with? Perhaps instead of judging that mom for looking so cute, you compliment her on how great she looks and work on the ugly parts of your own heart instead.

Let's put down the measuring stick of comparison. Allow yourself to be inspired by others and inspired by yourself. Praise God for the place you are in, whether that's in your darkest moment on the couch in a counselor's office just begging for some help, or walking through the grocery aisles in your stilettos feeling like a woman.

Don't allow yourself to be defeated by comparison or try to live up to something you're not, instead grow closer to Christ through inspiration of others and knowing that God made each of us in His image!

TODAY'S SCRIPTURE

"But the fruit of the Spirit is love, joy, peace, patience, kindness, goodness, faithfulness. Gentleness and self-control.
Against such things there is no law."
Galatians 5:22-23

I have friends who are incredibly peaceful people. They are calm, never gossip or raise their voices or get upset. Honestly, I worry about them sometimes. I have a tendency to be a bit feisty. My house is loud and out of control most of the time. I lose my temper at my kids more than I'd like to admit. Peaceful isn't really a word I could proudly put on my resume.

I love watching those "peaceful" women and I'm inspired by them. But what about the rest of us? You know, us with emotions, hormones, and a bit of a temper? I read stories in the Bible about women like Esther, Hannah, and Mary. They all seem so peaceful and calm. So, what's wrong with me? Why can't I be more like that?

We, yes, us modern, opinionated, stubborn women can be peacemakers, too. God calls us to it.

Remember those fruits of the spirit you learned about in Sunday school a million moons ago? Those still apply. I know, surprise, surprise, they aren't just for our kids. WE are to be love, joy, peace, patience, kindness, goodness, faithfulness, gentleness, and self-control in our home and in our relationships. This doesn't say you have to lose your personality and be boring. But think about how great it would be to put that stubbornness into good fruit? I parent a "wild one" as I affectionately call her. Stubborn is her middle name and I pray every day that she learns to focus that in a mighty way. Because God created every stubborn bone in her body, and when she learns to focus those wild bones on Him, she will do mighty things.

And you can do mighty things, too, sister. In all of your feistiness and wild personality. You can be a peacemaker. A kindness giver. A faithful friend. A gentle spirit. A joyful woman. A loving wife. Yes, even a patient mom. You can be all of those things because you are His and He has made you new.

In the midst of your chaos today, remember that God created every feisty bone in your body.

He wants to use it for His glory and will show you the way to be a peacemaker! Focus on those fruits of the Spirit today and ask God to fill you with each of them.

RESPONSE

PRAYER

111

TODAY'S SCRIPTURE

" 'Come to me, all you who are weary and burdened, and I will give you rest.' Take my yoke upon you and learn from me, for I am gentle and humble in heart, and you will find rest for your souls. 'For my yoke is easy and my burden is light.' "
Matthew 11:28-30

I see you. I hear the moaning of your heart and the exhaustion in your voice. I know the thoughts that go through your head as you survey the disaster that somewhat resembles your home. If I could cup your tear-stained face in my hands, I would tell you that you are mighty and strong. I would remind you that underneath the exhaustion you are a beautiful woman and you can do this. Every bit of the exhausting and trying journey of motherhood. You are not alone, you've GOT this.

Not only do I see you, HE sees you. The God of the universe. The one who knit those children together in your womb or in your heart. And He wants you to know something so important about the grace and love He offers you.

You need REST.

True, honest, and real rest that only comes from the Savior of the world breathing life into you. No amount of coffee or chocolate bars you sneak from the year old Halloween candy stash will suffice or fill that void in your heart. No amount of away time with your girlfriends or date nights with your husband. Those things are all good things. Some of them REALLY good things (hello, Hershey's bar in the bottom of my purse). But none of them will ever fill your heart and revive your spirit the way Jesus can.

I know. It's EXHAUSTING. I'm at my wits end, the last straw, zero patience by about 9am every day. It's gloriously exhausting and wonderful work raising tiny humans. And Jesus knew that. He's not surprised one bit by your busy schedules, your tear-stained cheeks, or your cute clothes collecting dust in the closet. He knows your deepest fears, your hardest days, and your weakest moments. And He STILL loves you and wants to carry you through each and every day. He wants to give you true REST in Him.

So, are you going to let him?

I love the way the scripture in Matthew 11:28-30 reads in The Message Bible. "Learn the un-forced rhythms of grace. Learn to live freely and lightly."

If you're like me, life is anything but "free and light" most days. And grace? Grace at my house is so stinking forced you could cut through it with a butter knife. But Jesus wants to show us how to live totally free and be swimming in lavish pools of His grace.

We welcome you, sisters, to join us in rest. To find freedom in a peace that comes only from God and a kind of grace that only He can offer. Get away with Him and recover your life!

I AM Gentle and HUMBLE in heart

MATTHEW 11:29

TODAY'S SCRIPTURE

" 'Where is your faith?' he asked his disciples. In fear and amazement they asked one another, 'Who is this? He commands even the winds and the water, and they obey him.' "
Luke 8: 25

Where I grew up, I learned a thing or two about storms. From insane bipolar weather, to tornados ripping cities to shreds - never a dull moment. When you live in an area that is prone to horrific weather, you build a safeguard. Your home is built on a firm foundation, and you have a plan. It's just the standard of life when you live with the risk of storms.

We've been talking about building an unshakable foundation. One that can stand the test of time, that is built firmly on the word of God. But are you safeguarding for when the storms come? Because it's inevitable, the storms of life will come. It's easy to say you're unshakable when all is well, but we know that storms are coming or maybe you're in one now.

In Luke 8, Jesus is out on a boat with his disciples. A huge storm takes over and is filling their boat with water, threatening to pull them under. All the while, Jesus is napping. I've always found this story to be interesting because this was a quick storm. There were no meteorologists warning them a storm was coming, and they must not have seen any warnings in the sky. I imagine they set sail and it was sunny and out of nowhere, the storm came. A storm to test their faith. I took a trip to Israel a few years ago and got to sail on a boat across the sea of Galilee, the same place where Jesus calmed the storm in that boat. To my surprise, the Sea of Galilee really is just a small lake. You can see from one side to the other, so this storm really did catch them off guard because they wouldn't have sailed out had it been bad weather.

"Where's your faith?", Jesus asked them when they woke him.

How often do you hear that phrase whispered in your ear? How often do you walk out in the sunshine and you're hit by a storm out of nowhere that rips your faith away? Maybe you're battling the unthinkable. Your storm may be more than you think you can handle. You're begging God - "just wake up and rescue me!", and He's asking "where is your faith?".

Are you ready to stand fearlessly in your storm? Stand firm in the beautiful truth that Christ has already conquered them all!

RESPONSE

PRAYER

"We love because he first loved us."
1 John 4:19

It was a Sunday morning and I dropped my kids in their classes, walked in, and sat in the back of the room after worship had started. It had been one of those days and I was already beat. I sat in my chair, taking a moment to breathe and glanced up at the stage to see my husband leading worship (worth every hard moment of getting three kids ready for church alone to see that image of the man I love leading others to the feet of Jesus).

I must have looked frazzled when I walked in. It could have been the dirty hair or the spit up on my shirt. As worship ended and I sat back in my chair, a sweet woman walked over to me. She had watched me enter late. Saw me fumble through my giant diaper bag for a week old bottle of water to drink (that was probably the first in a week). She watched me cry through worship. She came over, gave me a hug, and put something in my hand, said "God bless you" and walked out the back door.

I looked down in my hand in the dark and could tell it was money. I couldn't see how much, but shoved it down in my pocket and wiped away the tears. God spoke to me in that moment about what it meant to show love. That to truly love others, even a complete stranger, is to show it. Our lives can be transformed by love. Love is active, love is living and being the face of Jesus to a stranger. Love is showing grace to your husband and kids on a hard day. Love is going a little farther and doing a little extra for those around you.

Love is God. God is love.

As I walked out of church that day, I slipped the wadded up money out of my pocket to see a wrinkled five dollar bill. Not enough to pay the electric bill or buy a package of diapers, but enough to teach a major lesson in love to an exhausted mama. A lesson I will always carry with me and remember when I show love to others. That $5 still sits in my wallet as a reminder of love.

Look around you this week. How can you show love to another by your actions and your words? A simple action of love could impact someone for the rest of their life!

We love each other
because HE
loved us first

JOHN 4:19

KARA KAE JAMES

Kara-Kae James realized early on in motherhood that we can't do life alone and desires to see women walk in their full potential as moms, wives and daughters of Christ. She fell in love with the written word at a very young age and loves encouraging others and pointing them to Jesus through story. She's married to her favorite pastor, Brook, and together they are raising four children and are passionate about adoption and creatively reaching people for Jesus! Kara-Kae is the founder and Executive Director of Thrive Moms and also writes and speaks about motherhood at karakaejames.com.

@karakae.james | @thrivemoms

www.karakaejames.com

JOY KELLEY

Hola friends! I'm Joy, a Chilean girl that after falling in love, abandoned the city life of Santiago, Chile to start a new one in the gorgeous southern California mountains. I feel so blessed to have an amazing husband by my side, a cuddly furry companion and an adorable baby boy that we welcomed 10.11.12. I am an Industrial Designer from the Universidad de Chile by degree, but I am in love with design in every shape and form. I've always loved expressing myself creatively, so sewing, crafting and designing came as a natural way to create.

@howjoyful

www.howjoyful.com

paige tate & co.

WE ARE PASSIONATE ABOUT INSPIRING
CREATIVITY
IN EVERYONE.
WE SIMPLY PROVIDE THE BEAUTIFUL CANVAS
TO IGNITE THE
spark!

FIND ALL OF OUR PRODUCTS AT

www.paigetate.com

AND FOLLOW US ON INSTAGRAM AT

@PAIGETATEANDCO